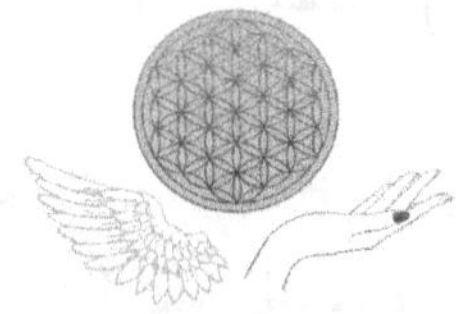

www.magentsunhealing.com

Email: chloemmoers@gmail.com

Intro

I wrote this book 3 days before Thanksgiving of 2020 because I realized I couldn't just sit around and witness another massacre of over **46 million** turkeys who were enslaved and then brutally killed just for a holiday. I could no longer be a bystander.

Ironically, this holiday is called "Thanksgiving"; implying gratitude. How can gratitude be celebrated at the expense of millions of lives? Let us not forget the genocide of natives as well, covered up by lies and deceit.

This book takes you on the experiences of a turkey from her birth to her death on a factory farm, a true account of life.

Her life was created and taken without thought to her soul. I intend to honor her soul and spirit, along with every other being taken by the hands and apathetic minds of humans. I hope you do so with me.

Turkey farm, MA. The year is 2020.

Table of Contents

Week 1

Day 1

I am born. Where am I? I do not know this place or understand it. It feels strange to me. I want to know where I am. Am I alone?

No. I am not alone. There are others like me, others around me. There are many, in fact.

I feel as though I am missing someone or something. There are others who sound just like me but they are not me. Something doesn't feel right. Who brought me here? Who brought me to the shell so that I could come out of it? That is who I am missing. I am missing whoever put me in the shell.

I feel sleepy, very sleepy, and a little happy or excited but I can't tell which one as both emotions feel practically identical to me.

I decide to look around. There are over 20 beings who look similar to me right next to me and many other shells and eggs that are

still intact. There is a lot of noise. The others
will not be quiet but I don't blame them.
I feel myself making the same sounds that
they are. It feels automatic as if I didn't start
making them, they just came. I don't
understand any of it yet, it all just feels in
motion without me contributing anything to
it.

I hope to find the one I am looking for
although I am still not certain who exactly
that is. Whoever it is, I miss them and feel
sad and uncomfortable without them yet I
do not know who they are.

Day 2

Pain. I feel pain. What is that? I cry out louder. I don't understand what is happening. I am picked up by a semi-warm fleshy gripping blob who has yellow on his head. He throws me. I land and my left-wing hurts. It is bothering me. What just happened? Who was that and why did that happen? I feel fear. The third emotion I have fully experienced is fear. I feel things strongly but cannot feel multiple emotions at once.

Day 3

I am alone. It is dark. It is so very dark. I feel sleepy. I am warm but there is a breeze. I want to sleep. Is it safe? I don't know but I have no choice but to sleep.

Day 4

What is happening to me? I am being taken somewhere. I am being hung upside down by my foot and now I am being forced between metal bars. My wings are flapping beside me. I have no grip. My beak. What is happening to it? What is happening to my face? I cannot stand this. I cannot hold myself up. Pain. More pain. So much pain. No beak. My beak was cut. I saw it leave me. There is so much pain. It hurts. Help. Someone help. I am in pain. I cry out and no one answers. No one helps.

I am thrown and it is dark again. So very dark it is. I feel sleepy, oh so very sleepy and tired. I am in a bigger space than before with many crying ones of me but soon there is practically silence as we fall asleep, some standing and some laying. We fall into a light and terrified slumber, restless yet relaxing.

My beak still feels pain. The pain isn't stopping. I need a break. I now feel a

combination of physical and emotional pain.
I didn't know that this was possible.

Day 5

Awake. I am awake. The light is dim and there is not much entering. There are no windows, just overhead lights. The lights are close to me but not close enough to touch.

Gentle. I feel a gentle touch. Someone is cuddling me. Someone is up against me. She feels so good. She feels so warm and loving. I wish to cuddle her back. I rest my head against hers. She is so soft. She coos and speaks softly to me.

My attention is no longer on the pain I am feeling. Instead, it is on her. I feel something new. It is warm, it is tingling and it is gentle. I feel hope and I feel love. We have imprinted on one another.
She is so very beautiful and caring. She makes me want to shelter a wing on top of her body. I don't understand why but I feel it strongly.

We spend time cuddling and exchanging
warmth and tingles and then she stops. She
is hungry. There is food. It tastes good but it
makes us feel tired. The lights turn off and
we sleep.

Day 6

Blue. I love the color blue. It is so beautiful. There is a large breathing blob that comes to dispense food. It is covered in a blue swaying object that smells like nothing. This blob is rough and sometimes kicks some of us. This can be painful and sometimes upsetting. I do not enjoy or like the blobs but I understand that they have some positive purpose even if it is not much. The only part of them that I enjoy is the food.

I like food. It makes me happy to eat it although I always feel tired after eating, I just don't understand.

Why do I sleep after I eat? Why do I feel the need to eat, to begin with? It is all so strange. I hope one day I will understand life more because for now, it is so confusing.

Day 7

Today I want to run. I don't know why but I really really want to run. It seems like it would be so much fun. My legs hurt. They feel cramped and I feel that they and I would be happier if we could move. I let my friend know this. She wants to run too. Now the issue is, how can we run? There is really not a lot of space and it is very dim light-wise. There is barely any light and I do not see well without light.

I preferred the light of where I came out of my shell. There, at least I could see properly.

All the others block the running space. I don't think we will be able to run. This is unfortunate and it makes me very sad. I wish I could see more and I wish we could play because that would be so very fun and nice.

I guess for now we shall cuddle and sleep.

Week 2

Day 8

The only time I see genuine light is when the blue blobs come in. When they come in they create a very bright pathway behind them. It always mesmerizes me. I get excited to see the light but afraid to see the blue blobs. Although the blue blobs may look pretty, they have injured many of us by throwing us, stepping on us, dropping things on us, and even throwing things at us.

I would say that at least 2 of us die every day from things related to the blue blobs. There are quite a lot of us here. 2 may not seem like much but it feels like a lot.

Whenever I see one of us dead, it makes me feel very scared and uncomfortable. It makes me panic and when I do I try to peck at whatever I can but I have no beak tip to do so. I always end up resorting to going towards my friend instead for comfort but when she is stressed then sometimes I panic, run into something, sometimes eat then pass

out or just pass out from running into the
wall or feeder.

Channelers note: Lilly's friend is named Tu.

Day 9

I don't like it when the blue blobs talk because when they do, it is very very loud and hurts both my ears and my emotions. They just never seem to be happy.

Tu seems to be feeling down. She hasn't woken up fully today. She opens her eyes occasionally but she refuses to eat or get up. This makes me feel very nervous. Why is this happening? Will this be forever? Will this happen to me? Can I do something to help her? How can I help her? There has to be some way.

I decide to stay by her side as much as possible today and so I eat a little less than usual but this is okay. I ate something small but as long as I eat then I will be okay.
It took longer than usual to fall asleep but eventually, I did. I think I need more practice on how to relax. Maybe if I got more practice then I would be able to sleep and feel better.

Day 10

I don't like being awake too much because being awake is painful. If I am asleep then there is no pain really and this is really nice.

Tu is still not feeling well and she does not smell well either. I am very concerned for her. I don't know how to help her but I really want to. There must be a way that I can. There is always a way to help.

I bring food to her. She won't eat it. I lay with her, pressed up against her. She accepts my warmth but not any food. She has not had water yesterday or today. Something is very wrong.

I feel helpless.

Day 11

Tu is dead. She won't open her eyes and she stopped breathing. She is laying there. She is lifeless.

I feel broken. The love I felt before feels broken. In many ways, this is worse than when I had my beak cut but in some ways, it is easier. I don't feel physical pain but I feel so much internally.

I don't understand my feelings and I don't know how to share them with the world. For now, I will just feel and be. I will sleep. I won't eat today. I can't. I also can't get too skinny. The weak ones are smaller and they die easier here. They are crushed easier.

The big ones of us here are favored by the blue blobs. They are nicer to these ones. I don't know why but I do know that I will only refrain from eating today, not tomorrow or the days after that, hoping that I will have days after that. Or maybe I shouldn't have

more days. I am not happy. I don't like living
without love.

Day 12

Today is lonely. I don't want to be social right now. It doesn't feel right.

It does get a bit chilly at night so I keep close to the other ones to get some extra warmth. I don't want to touch them right now but eventually, I just fall into the warmth and nice feelings. It is hard to resist.

Day 13

I wake up. I am still alive. I don't feel hope but I want to. Instead, I just feel sadness.

Is this how I am supposed to live? Is this how I will always live? I want more than this.

The death of Tu makes me feel such deep sadness and isolation. I most likely will die soon too. I feel this. I know this. No one can truly tell me different.

I think every being here knows that they are close to death. I don't think any of us have hope anymore. Why should we? Nothing lets us know that there could be good in our life.

Day 14

I feel ill. My bones hurt. My body aches. My weight puts too much strain on me. I feel beaten down. I feel like I am growing and expanding too fast for my bones, body, and soul to support me.

Every day is becoming increasingly more difficult. What should I do? I do not know.

I spend the rest of the day trying to sleep although it is not hard considering it is always dark where I live.

I watch some of the ones I live with being taken out of here into the light entrance by the blue blobs. They are taken upside down by 1 or sometimes 2 legs. They scream and flail. Sometimes, one of their legs or a wing is twisted in a way that doesn't seem right. This makes me feel faint when I see this.

I am lucky to not be picked up and broken like that.

Week 3

Day 15

How do I go about today? I don't know. I don't know how to feel or what to do.

I think I should socialize even though I feel no motivation to do so. Honestly, I rather sleep than do anything else. There is almost no light inside and I just don't feel the motivation to be awake. If anything, it feels like a burden to be awake.

I think I will sleep for now. I just don't want to face today. I don't know how to or even if I should.

Day 16

I smell something new, something I have never smelt before. It smells so good, so sweet, so pleasant. I want to eat it but where is it coming from? I don't think it is from the blue blob that has entered my space. They usually smell like nothing.

Maybe the blue blob brought it in? That would make sense considering I smell it here now but I didn't smell it before they entered the space.

Soon the smell leaves. I never found out why it was here or how it arrived, just that it had happened, yet almost as soon as something beautiful came, it left.

Day 17

Blue. An opening is created in the place in which I sleep and eat. This opening is separate from where the blue blobs come in. From where the blue blobs come in, I only see light but no color. There is not enough time to see anything but a moment of light.

Now there is blue. This is coming from another place that I haven't noticed before. The blue is beautiful. It is like nothing I have ever seen before. It's so much stronger than anything I have seen on the blue blobs. This blue feels infinite. It is above me, above all of us and it looks endless. There are also white, uneven shapes in the blue.

Is this even real? I don't know. I don't understand where this came from but I feel mesmerized. I feel so connected to what I am seeing.

I take a moment to look around, at all the ones similar to me. I see them so much more clearly now. We are so dirty. Some of us barely have feathers. I see all the bodies. Some are decaying and some are fresh. Along with the bodies, I notice how our food looks. It has very dull colors but a variety of them, primarily yellow-based.

The water we have to drink is clear but has spots of dirt and food in it. The ground is covered in feces but it does get cleaned up from time to time.

The walls are dark grey and full of scratch marks and there are even some dark red dots sprinkled in some spots.

The blue is gone and so is my sight. I don't know what happened but it has left.

Day 18

Silence. I wish to have silence. It is never quiet here, at least not completely. There is always someone awake and making noise or someone injured and crying out.

Light. I wish to have light. I want to experience joy and vision. I want to see new colors and different forms of the colors. I wish to experience more. I feel so curious about the world yet I am banned from exploring it. I want to know what is outside and I want to be awake and alert more.

Freedom. One day I hope to be free from here whether that means being let out and experiencing the endless infinity I saw in the blue or whether that means dying. Either way, I am willing and wanting to experience it as long as I no longer have to live like this.

Love. I miss feeling love. I felt love for Tu. Love gives me purpose and without it, I feel hollow and alone.

Day 19

I did nothing today. I slept and slept some more. When I woke up, I ate and went back to sleep or ate then defected and then slept. I didn't want to be with my thoughts. My dreams were more pleasant.

I dreamt of the possibilities of the outside world and being a part of the infinite blue light. I dreamt that I was a part of the infinite blue and that I floated like the white uneven shapes that I saw.

Day 20

I tried to make a friend today. I connected to someone nearby. She seems to always be terrified. She shakes and sleeps less than the others. She never seems to be able to fully calm down. She is always anxious and struggling. She honestly seems to be handling this worse than me.

I walked over to her and pushed passed the others as we are very much pressed together. I used my sense of smell and touch primarily and made my way to her.

At first, she closed her eyes and tried to condense herself to appear small but I tried not to make myself appear threatening and I think she understood that and so instead of being afraid and condensing any longer, she allowed curiosity to come out and she looked at me. She stared into my face with big eyes and observed me.

I observed her back and spoke to her. She spoke back and from there, trust and a friendship started to bloom.

Day 21

My new friend (Katrina) is very beautiful. She does have some missing feathers but besides this, she seems to be very nice looking.

I am not attracted to her necessarily but I can notice her beauty. We can find each other beautiful of course.

She is still a bit scared of me even though I try to approach her gently. She stood out to me because she is different from the others. She feels different and she pays close attention to her surroundings. She is very in tune with how others are feeling which I think causes her great fear and distress but also makes her a good ally.

She can sense when something is wrong and she can also sense who to trust. I'm happy to have found her.

She knows to trust me but she definitely senses my fear. I feel sorry for her but I also

feel compassion for her. I hope we can
snuggle soon.

Week 4

Day 22

Love. I am starting to feel love for Katrina. She is kind to me and keeps a watch for when I sleep. She doesn't sleep much but she does enjoy cuddling.

We lean against one another frequently. I tried to put my wing around her but she didn't seem to like that so I just resorted to remaining as closely pressed up against her as possible.

She shakes a little less now that I'm here but she prefers when I'm awake. When I'm asleep I think it makes her nervous because I can feel her shake more. Maybe she thinks that something will happen to me or maybe she gets terrified that she will end up falling asleep. I don't know exactly but I've been trying to stay awake more but it is hard due to the everlasting darkness.

Day 23

Freedom. I have escaped. I have left this horrible place finally! Katrina is beside me and we are in this beautiful open place. There is blue everywhere and even a new color, green! Soft green is below us. It feels so good and gentle. I feel so content sitting in this place and looking up.

When I look up, I feel so whole and so light. I feel no pain in my body or my mind. My emotions feel clear and I feel amazing! I feel better than I ever did before. Mesmerizing. This place is mesmerizing.

There is no blue blob insight. There is no one to get in the way of my joy and my love.

I think I see Tu! She is in the distance but she is flying! Wow. She is flying! This is amazing. I am so very happy for her. I can't believe she is doing this. I can't wait to be flying too one day.

Maybe I can fly? I will try. Nope. Can't fly yet. Even though I can't fly, I am still grateful that Tu has the opportunity to do so. This makes me feel happy for her.

Day 24

I am inside my walled prison. There is no escaping unless I die or am close to death. Yesterday didn't happen. Yesterday was in my mind. Today is real. This horrible life I am living is real. I don't even know how it's possible. I feel so depressed being here and being in this current situation.

I can't think of a way out. I don't think there is a way out for me. Maybe this is my fate.

Day 25

Sadness. I feel waves of sadness and grief within my body with no way of escaping it. I don't know how to deal with it, how to process it, how to be okay with the fact that I have lost so much and gained so little. I just don't understand what the point is.

What is the reason that this is happening to me?

Day 26

The way I think is in feelings and visuals primarily, with some sounds and vocalizations within my head.

I wonder if the blue blobs think or if how they live is automatic? I don't understand them or how they operate. Does death not bother them? They see it so much just as I do. I would think it would bother them.

Also, do they even have any thoughts of letting us out? Letting us be free? Do they even know that we are alive? They treat us like we can't feel. They treat us like we are lifeless, even before they take the life out of us.

I wonder why they do this and how many of them exist on the outside. Maybe they are forced to do this? I can't imagine them wanting to hurt us, but who knows. I truly don't understand these creatures and I don't know if I even want to. Maybe the answers to

these questions would hurt me more than
not knowing.

Day 27

Pain. I wake up from pain. Someone is attacking me. She is slightly bigger than me and she is slamming her wings at me and trying to peck me.

We don't have long enough beaks for her to succeed but this also means that I cannot protect myself.

I can't run as I don't have enough space. I try to kick her and flap her hard with my wings but this seems to aggravate her more. This is pointless. I am not winning and she is getting angrier.

Something feels off about her. Her skin feels different and her eyes appear different although I can't see them well. She is ill. I don't think she understands what she is doing. I don't think she wants to hurt me but I need to defend myself.

Katrina notices what's happening and she starts to help me. She ends up hurting the one attacking me a little and when this happens, finally she backs off and goes away.

I feel grateful for Katrina and sorry for this poor being. We suffer so much. This wasn't her fault.

Day 28

Katrina seems to be more on edge since the situation that happened yesterday. It seemed to have traumatized her. She has been through a lot and anything added on puts her into panic mode. I don't know how to help her so I just bring her some food and try to talk to her and lean against her.

She is shaking hard but with time she calms down and eventually falls asleep. I rarely see her sleep.

The sleep doesn't last long but it seemed to help her.

Week 5

Day 29

I feel extra tired and drained today. I don't understand why but I feel myself being dragged to the floor.

My body feels heavy. My muscles and bones ache and my head feels bigger than it's meant to be.

Maybe I pushed myself too much yesterday or maybe it is the lack of light.

Do I need light to live? I really don't know but if I do then I may pass soon. I accept whatever happens to me.

Day 30

I am alive again. I feel disappointed about this. I was hoping that I would stay in a sleep state forever. It is more beautiful and pleasant than here.

If I do pass soon then I hope I am asleep when it happens and I hope to not be afraid. If I pass during a time of fear I think that would result in issues. I don't know what issues but I know it wouldn't be beneficial.

Today, I spent the day thinking of what it's like to pass over. "Will it be like sleeping? Will everything just be black or maybe white? Will there be color? How will I feel? Will I feel anything at all?" These are some of the questions I thought about today.

I think that it will feel like I am being cuddled in a blanket of blue and white.

Day 31

I feel joy. We received a special food today and it tasted really good. I didn't know that food could taste that good. Usually, the food we eat is okay but it becomes bland the more I consume it.

This is special and it even has multiple flavors and textures! I have never had this before. When the door opened and closed from the blue blobs, there was momentarily some light and so I could see the food.

It has multiple colors. Green, orange, red, yellow, and even purple. I love it! I don't understand what I'm eating but it tastes fresh! It tastes like the smell of light.

Katrina was happy to eat it too. She consumed it fast. Everyone consumed it very fast which created some fights.

Luckily, I avoided the fights by only taking my share and then stopping. The ones who were more greedy were also more aggressive towards others and the ones who were more aggressive towards others received more aggression.

Eating this was the highlight and only real upside of the day.

Day 32

I feel good today after waking up. My head feels nicer and so does my body. I think the food really helped me.

I hope that we receive this special food every day. It makes me feel so much lighter and happier!

Even though it is dark inside, I feel light within my body today.

Katrina seems to be having the same response. She keeps chirping and interacting with me more calmly but with a boost of happy energy instead of fearful energy.

I didn't know that there could be such a shift in feeling from just food.

Unfortunately, we received bland and heavy food today. I didn't even want to eat it so I just pecked at it. I didn't have very much because I don't want to feel heavy again but

it felt like as soon as I took a single bite, I
was weighed down.

I feel sleepy. I shall rest.

Day 33

I feel terrible again. I hope to try something new today but there is nothing exciting to do. I don't have room to run or play. My feet hurt and ache and my body does too.

I am becoming more and more restless with every passing moment. Hopefully, I will be able to find something interesting to do at some point.

The most interesting thing that I can guarantee is my dreams honestly.

Day 34

I feel myself floating downwards, rocking back and forth, back and forth, continuously, like it's never-ending. It feels so soft and smooth.

It feels like I am being hugged and caressed by a huge and beautiful being who is unconditionally loving me and keeping me safe from the world in which I live.

My mind is only filled with this slow, descending, and swaying being and her love. I feel no attachment to the world, no feelings of loss or pain, just love, just warmth, just comfortability.

It feels so nice and continuous. I could be here forever and ever. I want to be here infinitely. I want to have no worries, no fears, and no pain, but it's only a dream.

Day 35

Is there any way that I can escape? Sometimes the blue blobs leave the light entrance open for a few seconds longer than usual. If I managed to be there, right by the entrance at the right time then I could try to escape.

I am worried though. What would happen if I were to be caught? Or if I get stepped on? Or kicked? Or if there is nowhere to go? Or if I can't run?

How will I even get over there? There are so many beings in my way. There are so many of us trapped here.

I don't think I can escape. I don't think it is possible for me to even reach the light entrance. My legs and patience would give out before I reached it.

I would be shoved out of the way and kicked by others like me, others who are afraid of living and dying.

I will try to think of a way out, a way of reaching the exit. Maybe it's possible.

Week 6

Day 36

Warmth. There is a strong feeling of warmth when I am holding and touching Katrina. My heart feels warm when we are together and so does the rest of my body.

I feel calm when I am with her. I can't handle the thought of us being separated.

The way I can tell that it is her is based on her smell, feel, and the unique way she speaks.

Each one of us has very unique ways of expressing our thoughts and feelings. We have different sounding voices. Certain things are common sounds like a call for help and hello but many sounds are unique to the individual.

I hope this makes us special but if everyone is like this then that's okay too. I do hope that there is something special and unique about us that is different from everyone else.

That would make me feel nice to know that
but there is no way of confirming it.

61

Day 37

Cold. I am so cold. There is barely any heat. The only heat is coming from one another. There is something wrong. I have never experienced such cold. The sick cannot handle this. I know many of us will perish.

I cannot tell what time it is. There is no difference between morning and night when there are no outside viewers. I cannot tell if we will get help from the blue blobs or if we will be left here to suffer and possibly die.

I think cold feels like death. When Tu died she was very cold. She no longer had a heart to beat and warm us both up.

Right now feels like the moment I lost her. The cold feels frightening and relentless. It feels like it is trying to take all of us with it. I continue to lay next to others. We are all working together to keep warm, even the ones who are ill are trying. We want to help

one another because by helping one another,
we helps ourselves.

Eventually after what I think is at least 3
hours the heat comes back and with it a
rattle. I forgot that the heat makes noise. I
guess I never noticed it before.

Time to sleep and separate from those who I
have not bonded with.

Day 38

I really don't know what to do today. It's very boring here. There are tons of us in a huge box with no colors for the most part and practically no light. The blue blobs just come to take bodies, torment us, and provide food and water, and the occasional cleaning but besides that nothing, literally nothing happens.

I'm getting tired of this. I just don't have the motivation to try to find things to do and so I just try to sleep.
I sleep most of my life. I eat, sleep, think and defecate. I cuddle sometimes and talk to Katrina but that is all.

Day 39

I smell something new again. This time it smells terrible. It smells like disease and blood. It smells so strongly of it.

One of the blue blobs has come near me holding at least 7 of my kind by either the throat or foot. They are floppy and dripping a greyish-yellow liquid and blood.

What happened to them? I can't take my eyes off them but at the same time, I do not want to see this horrible sight.

Even once they leave, the image won't leave my mind. Will that be my fate? Will that be the fate of Katrina?

Katrina looks healthy and she also is very round so I think she won't pass like this. The ones I saw were very slim.

Katrina gained weight quickly. When I first saw her she was much slimmer than now. I think I lowered her stress and that could be the cause of her weight gain. She has slowly started to eat more and more.

Day 40

Katrina keeps staring at me. She wants something. What is it that she wants? She keeps looking at me and then at her foot and back at me again.

Is her foot okay? She doesn't seem to be in distress.

She wants me to get something for her I think. Now she's looking at someone who is carrying a large piece of a food pellet. She wants it.

I tell her no. She looks sad.

I try to run after the one with the food but I run into someone else very quickly and then I fall. Now my left foot hurts.

I limp back to Katrina and she is asleep. Now I am in pain and can't be comforting. I try to go to sleep too.

Day 41

My foot is still bothering me. I tripped over it hard yesterday. I don't feel like walking because of the pain so Katrina brings me food this time and we sleep next to one another continuously.

Day 42

I am so bored. I have run out of things to think about at this point. I feel like running hard and fast and maybe into something because at least that keeps my mind focused.

Right now it is so hard to keep my mind leveled. I feel restless and uncomfortable. I don't want to do anything that I'm used to. I need something new. I don't want to live without something new. It's too much doing nothing all the time. I can't take it!

Week 7

Day 43

I am thinking and daydreaming about what happens after death. I think about death a lot because I see and feel so much of it around me. I can't always believe it to be real. So much doesn't feel real.

Who will find me after death? What will happen to my body and where will my mind go?

I get worried a lot of the time about my body. I don't know where the blue blobs will take my body after I pass and the idea of this terrifies me. I don't want them to take my body too far away from me. I don't know if this makes sense to others but it makes sense to me.

I want my body to go back to the place where it came from, wherever that is.

Day 44

Light specks shine in darkness. I had a dream about this. I had another dream where I was outside, but this time as I was peering at the sky. There was darkness, no blue, and no white uneven shapes. Instead, there was darkness like the kind that lives within my box but the darkness outside of my box was so much more beautiful. It was mesmerizing and it felt like it was calling to me, yearning for me to glide and fly towards it.

Within the dark abyss, there were dots of light everywhere. These dots were captivating, mesmerizing, and beautiful. They made me feel hope, hope that I haven't experienced in a long time. These dots felt like peace and relaxing freedom to me. They called to me and I flew towards them. I allowed my wings to carry my body.

My body felt as though it didn't even weigh a single pound. My wings carried the feathers

on my body and up we went. I landed in the
light and stayed there, surrounded by her.

73

Day 45

Katrina is feeling weak today. Her muscles are not very strong. She doesn't exercise or move much and she weighs very heavily. She looks abnormally big although the others around us do too.

I want to help her but I can't as we can't escape and there is no way to eat fresh and light food like before.

We are stuck in this cycle of feeling heavy, sleepy, and terrible. I just want it to finally end. I crave peace and connection back with the light.

Katrina looks at me with her beautiful large eyes and coos. She then closes her eyes and goes to sleep. I follow her lead.

Day 46

Tingles. My whole body is tingling. I feel a numb and tingling sensation flooding my whole body. I don't understand why and it is quite strange.

I wish to ask it to stop but I don't know how to talk to my body. I try to talk to it but it doesn't listen to me.

It doesn't feel too bad, it is just odd. It makes me worried. Will I die now? How do I know if I'm about to die? Will I know?

I don't think Katrina is feeling what I am. She just aches, but she looks at me concerned and begins panicking. She's worried about me. I don't want her to worry. I think I'm okay. I think I'm also ill. I think I can be okay and ill at the same time but I don't know honestly.

It's time to sleep because that's the only thing I could think of that may help.

Day 47

I tried my best to sleep all day. The days are getting longer and feel like they are fading into one. It's beginning to become easier and easier to sleep for longer and longer. It feels like my life is more real when I am dreaming than when I'm awake.

Day 48

I love you, Katrina. I love Tu. These are the ones in my life for whom I still feel hope towards. Even though Tu is dead, her energy still influences me. I feel it around me, loving me, guiding me, and aiding me.

Katrina gives me feelings of love and positivity still. I think that without both of these individuals in my life, I would be dusk of an individual. I don't think I could bear the thought of living another day. I would have tried to stop eating or trying to survive. I would have tried to go under the boot of the blue blob to be crushed.

But I can't do this. Katrina is still here. She depends on me. She's my friend. She would have so much anxiety and fear if I was gone. She would shake. She's not very social and so she probably wouldn't make another friend and I don't want that for her. We need each other no matter what.

Day 49

Do I have the ability to fly? I dream about flying all the time but I tried flying here and I wasn't able to. This saddens me.

Maybe I just need a running start first? If that's the case then I don't have enough room to run here in this box.

Hopefully, I can fly. If I can't then that would be very saddening. Flying sounds so beautiful and freeing. It sounds easier and more fun than walking or running.

Running and walking takes so much effort and sometimes it hurts my feet or puts too much weight on my heavy body.

If I can fly then I ask that before I pass, I will fly into the blue infinity.

Week 8

Day 50

Fruit. I dream of consuming something sweet and flavorful that makes me feel elevated and happy after it.

The food that is typically given to me is a little salty, fatty, easy to chew, and eat a lot of, but it is also very bland. It does not have much color or flavor. After I consume it, it makes me feel tired and heavy.

The food I consumed that one time made me feel light, airy, and happy.

I wonder how other foods would make me feel. Would something sweet make me feel love?

Would some foods make it feel like I am living a dream?

I am very curious about this. I hope to experiment with the foods I consume but I

cannot make this happen. I would have to
wait for it to happen to me.

Day 51

I feel grateful to have Katrina. Today I feel ill and bloated. My body feels too big to be handled upon my small legs. My muscles and bones ache and feel swollen. My head feels hot and heavy.

Katrina is spending time talking to me and helping me get through this. I truly don't know what I would do without her being there for me. She helps me grow and flourish and understands my needs and desires. It is truly a blessing that I never knew I would need so much.

Day 52

One of the blue blobs is very close to me. It is observing me through a shield across what I believe is its face. The reason why I think it has a face is that 2 eyes are looking at me. The blob appears to be angry and looks menacingly at me.

It grabs me and picks me up. I am upside down and my leg feels crushed. Pain. So much pain. I am thrown after being observed for a few moments and twisted around so the blob could get a full-circle view.

The throw brings me a few beings away from Katrina. I cry out to her to alert her to move away from the blob. She saw what happened to me and she distances herself to not be seen but her shaking will not stop. She cannot make them.

I lay there in defeat. I can't stand because of my leg. It doesn't look right. It looks crooked. I can't put any pressure on it.

After a few minutes, Katrina comes to me.
She had to find me and listen to my calls and
take her time. She is heavy and it is not
always easy for her to walk. She makes her
way through the crowd, towards me.

When she reaches me and touches me then
she finally stops shaking.

I feel better now that she is here and allow
myself to sleep through the pain.

Day 53

The pain has not ceased, if anything it feels worse. My leg throbs with every breath I take and I can't even think. I can't be quiet.

The pain is too harsh to be silent through it. It feels like calling out helps. It brings my attention to the outside world more than how I'm currently feeling.

Katrina looks very worried. She helps me limp to the food so I can have some but honestly, I do not want it. I am only having some to help me sleep and to get rid of the hunger. The hunger hurts me and I cannot handle anything else to bring me down.

Day 54

I am learning how to manage the pain and how to somewhat walk without putting much pressure on the foot.

Katrina has not been sleeping frequently to keep watch over me and I think it is affecting her once again. She's more fearful, similar to when I first met her.

I can't imagine what this would have been like if both of us had become injured. I don't know how we could have taken care of each other.

The pain only seriously bothers me when I try walking. Laying and resting is fine for the most part, it's just a dull throb.

I wonder how long it will be before the pain finally ceases entirely.

Day 55

Peace. I feel peace when I am asleep. I am so fond of sleep. Without it, I think I would go insane. I don't think I could stand the thought of living. Sleep gives me time to reflect and be away from the life of pain that I live and so for that, I am grateful for it.

Day 56

Time. I don't know how long it's been since my leg was twisted and snapped. I have no perception of time except for when the blue blobs come. I know that a certain amount of time has passed when they come in. They leave for long periods and come back again, always in a rhythm.

I don't know if time really matters. I think it keeps me focused. It lets me know that life continues forward and as long as it continues forward, there must be an end.

Week 9

Day 57

Friendship. Friendship keeps me from becoming a husk of a being. It makes me stay focussed on this day and on the next with something to look forward to.

I believe, I truly believe that friendship is what keeps Katrina and me from giving up.

I hope that everyone has a friend. Maybe the reason why so many of us have passed so early has been from lack of love. Love helps me heal. I can't explain how or why but I know it helps me heal. I have some control over my body and it knows whether or not I have a will to live and love gives me that will.

Day 58

I feel myself becoming increasingly more sluggish and tired. It is hard to keep eating, sleeping and healing. I have become more tired since my injury. I think my body is using my energy to heal instead of helping me in other ways throughout the day.

I don't have very much to do so I'm just daydreaming about the possibilities of the world outside of this box. I wonder how many of me there are and how many of the blue blobs exist.

Who exists outside us? Are there others that look completely different? I would assume that there has to be. It can't just be us or can it?

I want answers to these questions. Hopefully soon, I will have them.

Day 59

Yesterday I had the idea about if other creatures exist besides blue blobs and the ones who look like me. I've been thinking about this question a lot today when I'm not sleeping.

I think that there are others. I think maybe there would be creatures with different colors than me or the blue blobs. Maybe there would be yellow creatures who had blue feathers or white creatures with special food colors.

I don't know but I find this so very interesting. There are so many possibilities of things existing in the outside world, if only I was able to access this information and know for certain.

Day 60

My head feels like it is floating and spinning at the same time. I don't know what this means but I am okay with it. I am allowing myself to go in flow with these strange sensations.

As the day goes on, the sensations become stronger and stronger until eventually, I fall asleep. I don't even remember letting myself or noticing myself falling asleep. It just happened very instantaneously.

Day 61

So much light everywhere. There is light circulating around me, filling the space between me and you. The light connects me to you, Mama. It brightens us. You are dead. I feel you gone. I don't feel you near me. I know that you were the one who brought me into this world. I feel you and I don't blame you at all. I love you. I feel so much love for you. Rest In Peace Mama. I'll see you soon.

Day 62

I slept pretty much all day yesterday. I missed mealtime because I slept so much. I don't even remember seeing the blue blobs. Usually, whenever they appear, everyone wakes up and is on alert except for those who are very ill or dead so I am surprised they did not think I was either one of those and just step on me or shake me. Maybe they did shake me without me noticing. Who knows.

I don't think they shook me because if they did then Katrina would most likely be more on edge today but she seems calm.

My head also feels more clear and more balanced, but it still is heavy and hurts a little.

Day 63

Sugar. I taste sweet. The food today contains sweet! I am so happy! The sweet is intoxicating and I feel like I can't get enough of it. There is not enough food it feels for all of us today even there it looks like there should be more than enough. We are fighting over this food. It tastes delicious.

It looks a little different. It is more misshapen than our normal food but it is still in small pieces. I can't see the color as it's very dim in our box.

After I consumed all I could then I fell into a deep sleep and so did Katrina.

Week 10

Day 64

Loneliness is hitting me. It's not as much external loneliness as internal. I feel it deep within my heart. It drags on me and plagues me on a day-to-day basis. I try to suppress it and ignore it but it just feels constant.

Life feels unfulfilling. I feel that the blue blobs are using me for something and that something is not my purpose. I have a purpose much greater than them, than being used by someone.

I don't know what I will be used for but I have a feeling that I will be killed for my body by the blue blobs. I can't explain how I know this but I do. I know that they want my flesh and the idea of that is terrifying so I do everything I can to suppress it. I can't handle the thought of my flesh being given to them.

Day 65

Someone help me. I can't live like this much longer. It hurts. I feel so depressed, so down. I just want to die but I am scared of what will happen to me after I die. I don't want my body to be used. I want it to lay gently in the blue I see outside.

I am so scared. I am panicking. I need someone to help me. Please help me. I can't do this. I can't do this anymore. I am terrified. I am petrified. I feel lost, hopeless, and gone, yet I am not gone. I feel things and I am all too present. I don't know how much longer I can handle myself and these emotions. It is driving me to a point where I can't take it. I refuse to take even one more moment of it but what can I do about it? Practically nothing. Nothing.

Day 66

Gentleness. I feel a wave of love swarm around me. It brings my attention to bright and light colors.

I look down below and see the box in which I have lived my whole life. I see the ones who look similar to me from above. I didn't know that there were so many. It seems endless. I can't even tell which is Katrina.

A presence turns me to face upright once again. It is hard to keep my mind away from the box and the hardships that happen here but the presence feels so warm and loving. She wants me to look up and finally, I do and I give in. At that moment, I feel pure bliss.

I wake up and feel a mix of loving sedation and a disconnection from the boxed world where I live, eat and dream.

Day 67

Peacefulness is something that I want to live in constantly. Fear stresses me out too much.

I hate the smells here. They are so strong and horrible. The smells get bad to the point where I pass out. I can't explain it. The feces, death, and disease without any breeze or fresh air feel intoxicating to a point where I can't keep my eyes open.

I am thinking that that's why the blue blobs appear the way they do. It looks like the blue is a cover for something underneath. Maybe they look similar to us underneath but, I don't think so. They are too upright. It is in a way that makes me feel uncomfortable, at first it was even terrifying looking. They also have a very ill-proportioned face that doesn't rest well with me.

I wonder how they think I look. I wonder if I
will ever see how they appear underneath
the blue.

Day 68

Tiredness. I slept most of the day like usual and this time experienced very little and insignificant dreaming. The times when I am awake, I just think about sleep.

Day 69

Sometimes I have nightmares. I dream of Katrina being killed by the blue blob in front of me or her being taken away and never returned. Other times I think of living here infinitely, in a loop of endless misery, or being taken, killed, and eaten by the blue blobs.

In these dreams, the blue blobs always appear to look more terrifying. Their eyes become much smaller and they become taller and have claws. I hate seeing them. They always cause me to panic.

I hope to stop dreaming bad dreams and stick to the ones that give me something to look forward to.

I can't tell if I prefer being awake or having nightmares. Both I don't want to live through.

Day 70

Katrina has been sleeping more lately as well as eating more. She is getting increasingly bigger and less anxious.

Her body aches more but I think she eats away the pain. I understand how because when I eat, I also feel very distracted from everything else because my attention is only brought to that current moment. Also, when we eat we become increasingly more tired and that tiredness keeps us even more focused on the task at hand.

I do feel worried for her as sometimes I view the largest of us being picked by the leg or wing and brought outside with the other blue blobs. I don't know what happens to them, but they never come back and this terrifies me.

I try to let Katrina know to stop eating so much but it is only food and I that bring her comfort and she won't give up one of those things. It keeps her mind centered on something. I can't stop her.

Week 11

Day 71

I feel like I am slowly becoming more like the Katrina I met when we first became friends.

I have more anxiety, I shake more, I worry more but the only difference is that I sleep more than the past version of her. It's like we traded roles in many ways. I now try to watch over her the way she used to do for me although it's not the same because I sleep a lot.

We lean against one another to sleep so we can always tell if one wakes up and starts moving and when that happens then usually the other will follow. We try to stay together as much as possible and avoid all unnecessary separation. You never know what can happen in a time frame of even a few minutes.

We only separate if one of us feels ill to get food for them.

Day 72

I wake up to the sound of banging. There are more blue blobs than usual in here and they are making noise. I don't understand what they are doing but it is scaring all of us.

They are speaking to one another very loudly. It sounds aggressive. I truly don't understand what they're doing but it only becomes louder as the minutes pass.

They start pushing their top limbs against each other, hard. One falls and lands on some of us. This kills and injures the ones he lands on but he doesn't seem to care. Instead, he pushes the one who made him fall back, harder this time. This goes on for a little, hurting some of our wings from their feet in the process but a few more blue blobs show up and it immediately ends. They leave and we end up receiving food later than usual.

Day 73

I don't understand the blue blobs very much. I don't get how they could treat one another like that.

They already treat us terribly. Why would they want to also do that to each other?

The ones who were killed are still lying on the floor, and the injured ones are slowly dying. We can't help them, we can only watch and hope that they are not suffering, but it is clear that they are.

Day 74

It feels as though the lights are dimmer today, but it is not clear if they are actually.

It could just be my eyes as there is no real way for me to tell the difference.

I ask Katrina and she agrees, so I guess that it is something more than my eyes. I can't see her nearly as much as I usually can and the blue blobs don't seem to be fixing it. I assume that they are the reason for this as they always come in after there is a change in the box.

I don't know but I decide to sleep through it. Of course, there is nothing more to be doing.

Day 75

What do the blue blobs consume or maybe they don't eat? I can't always tell if they are alive like us or if they are something else.

The box I live in is not alive and it is cold and so are the blue blobs but I don't think they are not alive. I wouldn't say they are dead though. I hypothesize that they are just something else, neither dead nor alive but I have never seen anything besides my kind and them move so swiftly so I guess that means they are alive. There is just no way of verifying it.

Day 76

Blue is all I have been thinking of today. It's so beautiful and I miss it so much. When I saw it fresh that one time, it was one of the most beautiful moments of my life.

I love fresh colors to eat too, they always taste better.

Today, the lights are dimly there once again. It is no longer practically complete darkness. This is good because now I can see Katrina and my food and can do things properly, but honestly, I preferred sleeping in darkness that was almost complete. It just felt better to me and it was easier to sleep for longer.

Day 77

Sleeping and cuddling are my favorite hobbies. I do want to try something new though. I wonder what other possibilities exist to do outside of this box? There has to be more things to do, right?

I don't feel motivated to do much today like most days and so I go back to sleep almost as soon as I've woken.

Week 12

Day 78

I don't wish to call this place my home. I feel I have a home, just not here.

This is where I live but it will never be the place where I belong.

I think sometimes that everyone is brought into circumstances that are miserable to them, maybe mine is just prolonged. I hope that all suffering and pain ends at some point. If it doesn't then I really don't know what to do next in my life. I can't live with eternal suffering. Just the thought of it causes me extreme anxiety. I just have to trust that this will not be my fate. That is all I can do for now at least.

Day 79

I can't decide if it is beneficial for me to have hopes and dreams and be curious about the world because in some ways it gives me hope and helps me get through daily life but, in other ways it just makes me feel horrible about the life I live.

Day 80

I don't understand why this is all happening to me. It all feels surreal. Is it even happening? My dreams feel so real and the life I live does not unless something bad is happening.

Sometimes I can't make the distinctions between dreaming and being awake. The only reason why I believe that being awake is real rather than the dreams is because when I dream, my dreams are usually not consistent and this lack of consistency with lots of things I don't understand is confusing to me and very different from being awake but, in some ways being awake and the things that happen are just as confusing to me.

Day 81

Katrina seems to be doing better now. She is beginning to handle having the extra weight more now and is moving more even though we can't go very far.

It feels like the ones around us are becoming more and more restless and increasing in volume. They scream so loudly. I think they are ready to leave and can't handle the thought of being here any longer, just like me.

Day 82

I think that even if I tried, I wouldn't be able to sprint. I feel too heavy and my bones and muscles feel too weak.

I don't even imagine escaping anymore because there is no way to get to the exit and even if I tried, I wouldn't be able to escape. I can't move that fast. I am not capable of it.

I think when I was much younger, I could have run and had the energy for it but now, I can't even picture it happening.

Day 83

Death. There is more death than usual today. It is terrifying but also accepting. I don't know how to explain what this means. It is a feeling. I feel so much and these emotions just seem to get stronger with every passing day. One day they will get strong to a point where others can feel them too I think.

Katrina can always feel my emotions because her emotions change based on mine, even if I don't speak or make noise, she can always tell.

Katrina knows when I am having a bad dream or when I need comfort and she is always there for me. She is very empathetic and I would like to believe that I am too.

The death surrounding us is coming stronger than ever and I can't tell the reason why. I think it may be due to the stronger smells. Maybe these smells mean something that I

am unaware of. Maybe they bring more
illness with them.

Day 84

Am I special in any way or am I average? I want someone to give me an answer to this question besides Katrina.

I know that she views me as special because she chose me as a friend above anyone else but I want to know what others think too. I hope that I am special but if I am then I don't know how this can help me or make a difference.

Week 13

Day 85

I feel calm and sad today. I have a feeling that the end of my life is approaching. I can't tell who gave me this feeling or how I received it but I know that the end is near. Soon I will not be here. Soon things will be over.

Day 86

Nothing exciting happened today and I feel unhappy. I want something nice to happen for once besides dreaming.

Almost every day is the same here with the same events happening. We sleep. We are fed. We are sometimes kicked or pulled. There is darkness and only 2 moments of pure light when the blue blobs come and go. That is all. Sometimes there is fighting, sometimes we are more chatty or we go through times of almost complete silence.

The repetitiveness is just getting to be too much for me. I can't live doing nothing. I just can't.

Day 87

I can't remember the first moments of my life anymore. I can't remember how it started and how it felt. All I remember is getting my beak cut and then there was nothing after that. I also remember feeling lighter in weight and having more energy to move around and do more than sleep.

I wish I could have told my younger self some warnings but at the same time, I think it would have been too much for her to hear. I don't know what I could have handled back then or what I was willing to.

I guess I was meant to not know these things or maybe that's just the way it happened.

Day 88

My feathers keep shedding and falling in large chunks. I don't like having my skin exposed. It is not cold inside and so I do not feel cold as there is so much body heat but I do feel uncomfortable.

I wish I could pick up my feathers and place them back upon my body but unfortunately, I cannot and so for now I shall live with it because I have no other option.

Day 89

I never noticed how many of us barely have feathers. Most of us here have lost a considerable amount. The floor is littered with them. It creates a soft bedding for us but there is also feces on top of them which is not pleasant to lay upon. I hate touching my own feces. It makes me feel like I am never clean and I have no way of properly cleaning myself if I do end up getting some on me when I am walking or sleeping.

Day 90

Sleepiness. I feel so sleepy, more than usual. I can't keep myself awake for very long today.

Day 91

Katrina looks so beautiful and I notice myself staring at her frequently. I have a hard time not looking at her when I am awake. She is the only one whom I truly love. She understands me. She cares about me. No one else does.

Week 14

Day 92

I don't understand my feelings today. They are strong but very strange. I don't really want to be feeling them as they feel confusing. I don't like not understanding what is happening around me. I enjoy being aware of all aspects of my life.

I will try to explain the feelings I am experiencing. I feel dry emotionally and intense. I feel somewhat sad yet relaxed and almost sedated. I feel lost too. This is all mixed to create one complete emotion. I hope it goes away as it is rather uncomfortable. I don't like feeling uncomfortable.

Day 93

Freedom. I dream of freedom. I dream of being in a place where there are no restrictions, no walls, no fears, no uncertainties, no forced deaths, and especially no blue blobs.

I cannot wait for this if it is in my fate to have this happen. I hope it happens in one form whatever that may be. I really hope.

Day 94

I wonder if anyone can hear my thoughts or if it is just me experiencing them. I can't hear the thoughts of others but I can feel what they're feeling usually.

I can even feel what the blue blobs feel. Sometimes they feel anger, sadness, even fear, or once in a while they feel like nothing. I always find it strange when they feel like nothing. How is that even possible? I have never felt absolutely nothing.
I have felt numb at times but it never felt so blank. I think this feeling of blankness allows them to hurt us the way they do. I know I certainly couldn't hurt someone else like they do unless I felt absolutely nothing because if nothing is felt then no love or empathy can be felt either.

Day 95

Today was pretty uneventful. Katrina slept most of the day and so did I. It is so easy and simple to sleep life away. It makes time invisible but in a good way.

Sometimes when I think about my life's circumstances, it makes it harder when time plays a role. Time passing shows me that things are not getting better, no matter how much I want it to.

I wonder what others think of time.

Day 96

The end is closer. I can feel it. I am ready for it. I can't handle the suffering anymore.

My leg never healed properly. I can't put much weight on it or use it for the most part but I try not to think of it and just accept it because there is no point feeling things for something that I can't change, especially something that happened in the past.

I know that if I lived a life in which I was free and didn't have to worry or be afraid all the time then I wouldn't want to die. I would be happy living and continuing to move forward. I would be glad to experience another day and thank the blue infinity for it but unfortunately, I live a life that is painful and so I want this pain to end, no matter how that may be.

Day 97

Sleep has been my day and my night. For me, day and night are the same. There is no difference between them. Both are dark. Both are times of sleep and trying to forget.

Day 98

Something is happening. We are being exposed to the light. The blue blobs are here, more plentiful than ever and they are lifting us by our necks, legs, and wings and taking us out of the box.

I have never been out of the box before. I feel emotions mixed with excitement that I am leaving and fear for what may happen to me and Katrina. I am particularly worried about her because I love her and care for her more than myself.
I tell her I love her. We are picked up harshly by several blue blobs. She is picked up by her neck, and I by my non-injured foot.

It hurts my foot to be carried like this. The blue blob is holding it tight.

The outside is so bright. I have never seen so much. There is green. There is beauty everywhere. I love this so much. The air feels amazing. It brushes against my bare skin patches. It is cold but I don't mind. I just wish that I wasn't being carried painfully during this.

The infinite blue has grey patches in it and beyond that are grey boxes and green floors. I am mesmerized by the beauty for just a few moments. The light feels so bright for my eyes. It is hard for my eyes to not hurt but I don't mind the pain when it comes with this scenery.

I am shoved in a tiny metal box, pressed tightly up against others who I do not know. We all try to scream as we feel so cramped but it gets us nowhere.

I no longer have a view of the beauty. We are put in this tiny metal contraption, on top of a loud object. All I can see are others in similar metal boxes.

The loud object starts moving. I feel so cramped and uncomfortable. I am scared for Katrina. I call for her but she does not answer. I do not see or smell her. The air I do smell is pleasant but I no longer care.

I can't sleep away the uncomfortableness, the light, and other beings won't let me and so I wait it out. I wait and wait and finally after what feels like forever, it is dark. No more light and so I sleep. I am barely dreaming, just unconscious.

Last Day of Life: Day 99

There is light again. I wake up. My body hurts. The loud object stops and the tiny box where I am placed is moved. It is being carried by a naked blob with brown and green coloring on its torso, into a huge box. This box reminds me of my old one but it is much louder.

No, not again, make this torture stop. I don't want to be separated from Katrina and have to live my life in just another box. I need and I want an escape from all this.

I am roughly taken out of the box, hung upside down with my legs painfully hung on a cold piece of loud metal. The metal starts moving. There is water near me. I see the water.

Pain. The water brings pain that I cannot describe. It is torturous. It is too much. I can't. I can't. It stops my thoughts. It stops everything. It is pure, unstoppable pain. I am conscious but others around me are not.

I am still being moved along next to others by my feet. My throat. I am bleeding. So much blood. My mind is leaving. Pain. So much pain. It's leaving me. It's leaving me. It left.

Over 46 million Turkeys are killed in the USA for Thanksgiving alone. 300 million turkeys are killed every year in the USA in total with 99% living on factory farms. Please take a moment of silence for these sentient lives and please don't be the cause of their suffering.

About the Channeler/Writer

Chloe Moers is an Interspecies Communicator, Animal Reiki Master, and is the founder of Unconditional Love for All Reiki. She dedicates her life to saving the lives of farm animals. Chloe discovered her love for animals at the age of three and never consumed flesh. She connected to the spirits of animals who have passed at the age of five and saw their cruel deaths by connecting to their spirits. She was raised vegetarian and turned vegan at age fifteen. Currently, Chloe is creating a nonprofit to incorporate Reiki, Interspecies Communication, Recipes, and Vegan education to save billions of animals' lives.